Cooking with Rum

Made Simple

40 Rum Recipes That Will Amaze Everyone

BY: Valeria Ray

DELICIOUS
HOMEMADE
FOOD

Recipes

License Notes

A Special Reward for Purchasing My Book!

Thank you, cherished reader, for purchasing my book and taking the time to read it. As a special reward for your decision, I would like to offer a gift of free and discounted books directly to your inbox. All you need to do is fill in the box below with your email address and name to start getting amazing offers in the comfort of your own home. You will never miss an offer because a reminder will be sent to you. Never miss a deal and get great deals without having to leave the house! Subscribe now and start saving!

SUBSCRIBE

——— TO NEWSLETTER ———

https://valeria-ray.gr8.com

Contents

Cooking with Rum

MMMMMMMMMMMMMMMMMMMMMMMMMMMMMMMM

Chapter I - Boozy Beverage Recipes

MMMMMMMMMMMMMMMMMMMMMMMMMMMMMM

(1) Tropical Twister

Batten down the hatches, take control of the remote, sit back, relax and enjoy this delicious rum cocktail.

Yield: 1

Cooking Time: 3mins

List of Ingredients:

- Ice
- 1-ounce fresh pineapple juice
- 2 ounces light rum
- ½ ounce orange-flavoured liqueur

MMMMMMMMMMMMMMMMMMMMMMMMMMMMMMMMM

Methods:

1. Fill a cocktail shaker halfway full with ice.

2. Add the pineapple juice, light rum and orange liqueur to the shaker. Stir to combine.

3. Strain into a glass and enjoy.

(2) Black Pearl Shooter

One sip of this shooter and you will be transported to the seven seas aboard this ghostly galleon.

Yield: 1

Cooking Time: 2mins

List of Ingredients:

- ½ ounce grenadine
- 1 ounce blue curacao
- 1 ounce black rum
- ½ ounce cranberry juice
- Lemonade (to fill)

MMMMMMMMMMMMMMMMMMMMMMMMMMMMMMMM

Methods:

1. Add the grenadine, blue curacao, rum and cranberry juice into a cocktails shaker.
2. Shake it all about.
3. Strain into a sour glass and fill with a splash of lemonade.

(3) The Castaway Cocktail

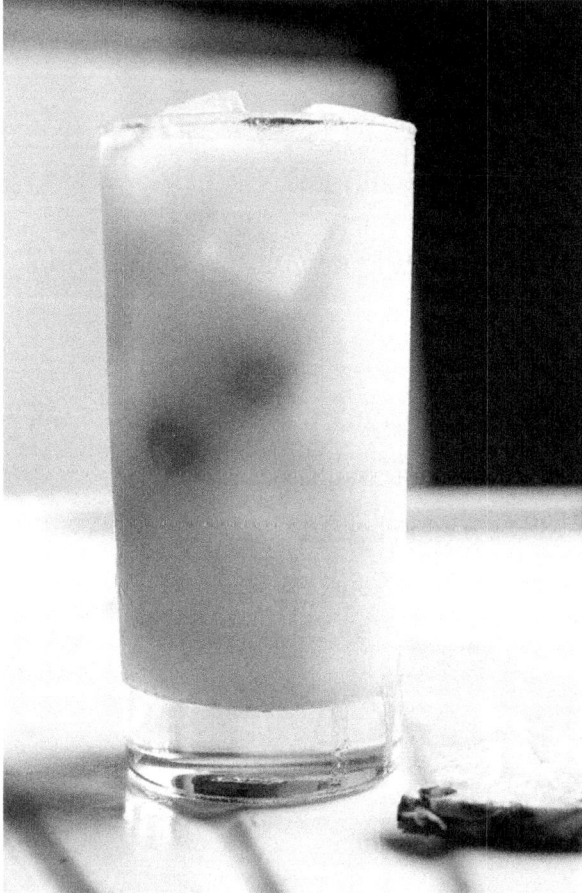

This perfect fruity rum cocktail will transport you to your very own Desert Island.

Yield: 1

Cooking Time: 3mins

List of Ingredients:

- 3 ounces coconut rum
- 2 ounces freshly squeezed orange juice
- 2 ounces banana juice
- 2 ounces strawberry mix

MMMMMMMMMMMMMMMMMMMMMMMMMMMMMMM

Methods:

1. Add the rum to a highball glass.
2. Next, add the fresh orange juice, banana juice and strawberry mix.
3. Fill the glass with ice and enjoy.

(4) Captain Jack Sparrow

Take care not to drink too many of these rum cocktails – you don't want to be three sheets to the wind!

Yield: 1

Cooking Time: 3mins

List of Ingredients:

- ¾ ounce rum
- ¾ ounce whiskey
- ¼ ounce coconut rum
- Splash freshly squeezed lime juice
- Ginger ale (to fill)

MMMMMMMMMMMMMMMMMMMMMMMMMMMMMM

Methods:

1. Combine the rum with the whiskey, coconut rum in an ice-filled whiskey sour glass.
2. Add a splash of lime and fill to the top with ginger ale.

(5) The Blackbeard

Edward Thatch from Bristol, England or Blackbeard as he became known was one of the most feared pirates of his time. This cocktail is named in his honor.

Yield: 1

Cooking Time: 2mins

List of Ingredients:

- 1 ounce spiced rum
- 1 ounce root beer schnapps
- Ice
- Cola (to fill)

MMMMMMMMMMMMMMMMMMMMMMMMMMMMMMMM

Methods:

1. Add the rum and schnapps to an ice-filled highball glass.
2. Fill to the top with cola and serve.

(6) Captain Kidd's Tipple

Captain Kidd, a Scottish sailor was accused of piracy and hanged in 1701. This boozy beverage is named in his honor.

Yield: 1

Cooking Time: 3mins

List of Ingredients:

- 1 ounce rum
- ¾ ounce crème de cacao
- 1 ounce gin
- 1 ounce Scotch whiskey

MMMMMMMMMMMMMMMMMMMMMMMMMMMMMMMMM

Methods:

1. Add the rum, crème de cacao, gin and Scotch to an ice-filled cocktail shaker.
2. Shake it all about and serve in a highball glass.

(7) Pirate's Grog

Loved by pirates everywhere, and guaranteed to put wind in your sails, Pirate's Grog is the perfect hot toddy.

Yield: 1

Cooking Time: 3mins

List of Ingredients:

- 1 shot dark rum
- 1 teaspoon sugar
- 2 cloves
- Freshly squeezed lemon juice (to taste)
- Cinnamon stick

MMMMMMMMMMMMMMMMMMMMMMMMMMMMMMM

Methods:

1. Add the rum, sugar, cloves, freshly squeezed lemon juice and the cinnamon stick to a coffee mug.
2. Top with hot water and enjoy.

(8) Crow's Nest

International Talk like a Pirate Day provides the perfect excuse to drink like one too!

Yield: 1

Cooking Time: 2mins

List of Ingredients:

- ½ shot spiced rum
- 2 drops of vanilla essence (divided)
- ½ shot coffee liqueur

MMMMMMMMMMMMMMMMMMMMMMMMMMMMMM

Methods:

1. In a tumbler, combine the rum, 1 drop of vanilla essence, coffee liqueur, remaining drop of vanilla. Stir and serve.

(9) Hot Apple Cider with Buttered Rum

Get the crew together and enjoy this strong and spicy rum infused hot apple cider with the rest of your shipmates.

Yield: 6

Cooking Time: 15mins

List of Ingredients:

- 2 quarts apple cider
- ⅓ cup butter
- ½ teaspoons allspice
- ¼ teaspoons ground cloves
- ⅓ cup brown sugar
- 1 cup dark rum
- 1 large apple (cored, sliced)
- 1 large pear (cored, sliced)
- 2 (2") pieces of ginger (peeled, sliced)
- 2 cinnamon sticks

MMMMMMMMMMMMMMMMMMMMMMMMMMMMMM

Methods:

1. Add the cider, butter, allspice, ground cloves, and brown sugar and bring to boil.
2. Turn the heat down to a simmer for 10 minutes, while occasionally whisking.
3. Remove the pan from the heat and stir in the rum along with the apples, pears, ginger and cinnamon sticks.
4. Serve.

(10) Frisky Wench

A drink fit for Anne Bonny! Irish pirate, Anne was a
notorious pirate from the 18th century, and sailed the seven
seas on Calico Jack's ship.

Yield: 2

Cooking Time: 3mins

List of Ingredients:

- 4 ounces spiced rum
- 12 ounces cranberry juice
- Lime wedges (to garnish)

MMMMMMMMMMMMMMMMMMMMMMMMMMMMMMMMM

Methods:

1. Divide the rum between 2 ice-filled Collins glasses.
2. Fill each glass to the top with cranberry juice, stirring to combine.
3. Garnish with a wedge of lime and enjoy.

Chapter II – Appetizer Recipes

MMMMMMMMMMMMMMMMMMMMMMMMMMMMMMM

(11) Salmagundi Salad in a Jar

Salmagundii is a meal thought to be served on pirate ships. It is a concoction of anything on hand and a type of pirate stew.

Yield: 6

Cooking Time: 20mins

List of Ingredients:

Dressing:

- 6 ounces preserved lemon juice
- 6 ounces extra virgin olive oil
- 1 teaspoon Dijon mustard
- ½ teaspoons sea salt
- Freshly ground black pepper

Salad:

- 1 rotisseries chicken (cut into bite size pieces)
- 6hardboiledd eggs (peeled, chopped)
- 2 ounces anchovies (diced small)
- 2 preserved lemons (juice extracted and reserved, julienned)
- 2/3 cup sweet pickle chips
- 6 ounces arugula
- 6 ounces baby spinach

MMMMMMMMMMMMMMMMMMMMMMMMMMMMMMM

Methods:

1. First, prepare the dressing. In a bowl, whisk the oil with lemon juice with the olive oil, mustard, sea salt, and black pepper. Combine until emulsified.
2. Next, divide the ingredients equally between 6 Mason jar.
3. Start with a layer of chicken.
4. Next, add the egg yolks, followed by the white, anchovies, julienned lemon, pickle chips, arugula, and baby spinach.
5. Screw on the lid and transfer to the fridge to chill.
6. When you are ready to serve, remove from the fridge and drizzle with the lemon and mustard dressing.

(12) Bermuda Fish Chowder

Fortunately, you don't have to venture into the Bermuda
Triangle to enjoy this chunky chowder.

Yield: 6-8

Cooking Time: 3hours

List of Ingredients:

- 6 rockfish heads
- 4 quarts water
- 1-pound onions (peeled, chopped)
- ½ pound peppers (diced small)
- ½ pound carrots (diced small)
- 1-pound potatoes (diced small)
- 1-pound leeks (washed, finely chopped)
- 6 ribs celery (trimmed, chopped)
- 2 teaspoons vegetable oil
- 1 (4 ounce) can tomato paste
- 2 teaspoons paprika
- 1 teaspoon tarragon
- 2 teaspoons curry
- 2 teaspoons thyme
- 2 teaspoons marjoram
- 2 teaspoons oregano
- 4 cloves garlic (peeled, minced)
- Salt
- 4 bay leaves
- 1 (19 ounce) can whole tomatoes (seeded, chopped)
- Ground white pepper
- ¼ cup rum

- ¼ cup sherry peppers or bird's eye chilli peppers

MMMMMMMMMMMMMMMMMMMMMMMMMMMMMMMMMM

Methods:

1. Add the rockfish heads to a pan of lightly salted, boiling water, until thoroughly cooked.
2. Remove the heads and set to one side to cool.
3. Through a fine sieve, strain the stock and set to one side.
4. Remove the meat from the fish bones while they are still warm and set to one side.
5. Sauté the onions, peppers, carrots, potatoes, leeks, and celery in oil until translucent.
6. Add the tomato paste and allow to sweat for a few minutes.
7. Pour in the fish stock, along with the fish, paprika, tarragon, curry, thyme, marjoram, oregano, garlic, salt, bay leaves, and canned tomatoes, bring to boil and allow to simmer for 2 hours.
8. While the chowder cooks, continually skimming off any surface scum and breaking up any larger size pieces of fish.
9. Season with sea salt, white pepper, rum, and sherry peppers.

(13) Rum, Maple and Pecan Topped Brie

A tantalizing combination of rum and melting brie, what's not to love?! The perfect appetizer to share with your shipmates.

Yield: 6

Cooking Time: 17mins

List of Ingredients:

- 3 tablespoons brown sugar
- 3 tablespoons dark rum
- 3 tablespoons pure maple syrup
- ½ cup pecans (toasted, chopped)
- 1 (8 ounce) wheel Brie cheese
- 1 (16 ounce) box gingersnapsp cookies (to serve)

MMMMMMMMMMMMMMMMMMMMMMMMMMMMMMMMM

Methods:

1. Preheat the main oven to 350 degrees F.
2. In a saucepan over moderate heat, combine the brown sugar with the rum and maple syrup.
3. Simmer until sugar is entirely dissolved, approximately 3-5 minutes.
4. Add the chopped pecans.
5. Add the brie to a casserole dish.
6. Pour the mixture on top of the Brie and bake in the preheated oven for between 6-8 minutes until the Brie is softened
7. Serve with ginger cookies.

(14) Butter-Rum Scallops

Unfortunately, pirates of old weren't lucky enough to dine on seafood but thankfully, times have changed, and these buttery scallops are sure to please even the most particular pirates.

Yield: 4

Cooking Time: 25mins

List of Ingredients:

- 2 tablespoons butter
- 1 pound bay scallops
- 2 tablespoons rum
- 2 teaspoons honey
- Sea salt and black pepper
- 1 (6 ounce) baby spinach
- 1 teaspoon fresh mint (finely chopped)

MMMMMMMMMMMMMMMMMMMMMMMMMMMMMMM

Methods:

1. In a skillet over moderate to high heat, heat 1 tablespoon of butter.
2. Add the scallops to the pan and cook, flipping over once, until seared for a total of 3 minutes.
3. Remove the scallops from the pan, leaving the butter in the skillet.
4. Add the remaining butter followed by the rum and honey and cook, while stirring until the butter entirely melts, approximately 60 seconds.
5. Return the scallops to the pan and season.
6. Cook, while occasionally stirring, for 60 seconds, to warm the scallops through.
7. Stir in the baby spinach and mint and cook until just wilted, for 60 seconds.
8. Serve.

(15) Rum-Glazed Shrimp and Mango

Tuck in me hearties, and enjoy succulent shrimp and exotic mango glazed in rum.

Yield: 6-8

Cooking Time: 1hour 5mins

List of Ingredients:

- ¼ cup + 1 tablespoon freshly squeezed lime juice
- ¼ cup dark rum
- 3tablespoons dark brown sugar
- 1 tablespoon fresh ginger (peeled, finely grated)
- 1½ teaspoons cornstarch
- 32 medium, tail-on shrimp (peeled, deveined)
- Sea salt and ground black pepper
- 1 firm, ripe mango (peeled, pitted, sliced lengthwise into 8 (1") thick slivers
- 2 tablespoons vegetable oil
- 12 ounces watercress (tough stems trimmed)

MMMMMMMMMMMMMMMMMMMMMMMMMMMMMMM

Methods:

1. First, prepare the glaze. In a pan, combine the ¼ cup of fresh lime juice with the dark rum, brown sugar and ginger, and over high heat, bring to boil.
2. Turn the heat down and while occasionally whisking, cook for a few minutes, until the mixture is slightly thickened.

3. In a bowl, whisk the cornstarch with 1 tablespoon of water, and stir it into the lime-ginger mixture. Cook while stirring for 30 seconds, until thickened. Remove from the heat and set aside to cool.

4. Divide and thread 4 shrimp onto 8 wooden skewers (soaked in water for 30 minutes before use). Season all over with sea salt and black pepper.

5. Thread the mango slivers onto 4 skewers, 2 per skewer and brush the mango and shrimp with the glaze.

6. Heat the grill to moderate to high, and oil the grill grates.

7. Arrange the seafood and fruit skewers on the grill and cook, flipping over once, until the shrimp are opaque and are blackened in spots; this will take between 3-4 minutes.

8. In a mixing bowl, whisk the remaining lime juice with the oil and season. Add the watercress, tossing to coat.

9. When you are ready to serve, evenly distribute the watercress between the 4 plates, topping each one with 2 shrimp and 1 mango skewer(s).

(16) Cinnamon Rum Glazed Cannon Balls

These meaty cannon ball meatballs glazed in cinnamon and rum are sure to hit the spot! Did you know, a little over five years ago a research team in North Carolina recovered the big guns from a pirate wreck? Blackbeard's cannon catch dates back over 300 years heralding the end of his pirate career.

Yield: 24

Cooking Time: 55mins

List of Ingredients:

Meatballs:

- 1-pound lean ground pork
- 3 rashers, raw bacon (finely minced)
- ¼ cup soda cracker crumbs (ground)
- 1 medium egg
- 1½ teaspoons cinnamon

Cinnamon Rum Glaze:

- ¼ cup butter
- 2 medium apples (cored, chopped)
- 1 cup dark rum
- 1 cup brown sugar
- 2 tablespoons green bell pepper (finely chopped)
- 2 teaspoons cinnamon
- 1 teaspoon crushed red pepper
- ½ teaspoons ground mustard

MMMMMMMMMMMMMMMMMMMMMMMMMMMMMMMM

Methods:

1. Preheat the main oven to 350 degrees F.

2. In a mixing bowl, combine the pork, with the bacon, cracker crumbs, egg, and cinnamon. Using clean hands form into 1½" balls.

3. Arrange in a single layer on a greased baking sheet and bake in the oven until cooked through, for half an hour.

4. To make the glaze. Over moderate heat, in a frying pan, melt the butter.

5. Add the apples and cook for a few minutes.

6. Add the rum and increase the heat, cooking until the sauce reduces by one half.

7. Stir in the brown sugar, along with the bell pepper, cinnamon, red pepper, and ground mustard. Bring to boil and boil for 60 seconds.

8. Add the meatballs, stirring to coat gently.

9. Skewer each meatball with a cocktail stick and serve.

(17) Rum and Cola Wings

Even Long John Silver would love these good n sticky wings with rum and cola.

Yield: 4

Cooking Time: 1hour 25mins

List of Ingredients:

- 2¼ pounds chicken wings (wing tips removed)
- 2 tablespoons smoked paprika
- 1½ teaspoons chili powder
- Salt and pepper
- Glaze:
- ½ cup dark rum
- ¾ cup cola
- 2 tablespoons honey
- ¼ cup red hot sauce
- ⅓ cup butter (chopped)

MMMMMMMMMMMMMMMMMMMMMMMMMMMMMMMM

Methods:

1. Preheat the main oven to 360 degrees F. using baking pape, line a large baking tray.
2. Add the wings to a bowl and sprinkle with smoked paprika and chili powder. Season with salt and pepper, tossing to evenly coat.
3. Lay the wings, in a single layer on a baking tray and bake until golden brown, for 45 minutes.
4. To prepare the glaze. Combine the rum with the cola, honey and hot sauce in a pan. Stirring to combine.
5. Over moderate heat bring to boil before reducing and cooking at a rapid simmer until the mixture easily coats the back of a spoon, this will take approximately 10 minutes.
6. A little at a time, whisk in the butter until entirely combined and transfer to a mixing bowl.
7. Allow the wings to cool slightly, before in batches adding to the glaze, tossing to coat.
8. Return the winds to the oven and cook for an additional 10 minutes, until they are sticky.
9. Serve and enjoy.

(18) Mini Pineapple Rum Shrimp Tostadas

The most famous Mexican pirate, Spanish born Fermin Mundaca, operated a contraband empire from Islas Mujeres off the coast of Quintana Roo during the mid 19th century. We are sure he would have approved of these juicy fruity shrimp tostadas.

Yield: 8

Cooking Time: 30mins

List of Ingredients:

Slaw:

- Cabbage (shredded)
- Freshly squeezed lime juice (to taste)
- Olive oil (to taste)

Shrimp Tostadas:

- 4 (6") soft flour tortillas
- ¼ cup brown sugar
- 1 tablespoon freshly squeezed lime juice
- 2 tablespoons rum
- 1 teaspoon taco seasoning mix
- 16 small shrimp (peeled, deveined)
- 1 small red onion (peeled, finely sliced)
- 1 cup fresh pineapple (chopped)
- 1 avocado (peeled, pitted, diced)
- ¼ cup cilantro (chopped)

MMMMMMMMMMMMMMMMMMMMMMMMMMMMMMM

Methods:

1. In a bowl, toss the shredded cabbage with the lime juice and olive oil. Quantities will depend on personal taste. Transfer to the fridge until needed.

2. Using a 2-3" circular cutter, cut 4 circles out of each of the tortillas, to yield 16 in total.

3. In a bowl, combine the brown sugar with the lime juice, rum, and taco seasoning mix. Add the shrimp, stirring to coat and set to one side for 12- 15 minutes.

4. Remove the shrimp from the marinade and grill on each side for 1-2 minutes.

5. Arrange the tortilla circles in a single layer on a grill and grill for 60 seconds on each side.

6. Arrange the red onion, pineapple, and diced avocado on a grill pan, cooking until just browned.

7. Arrange a small amount of the slaw on the tortillas and top with the pineapple and avocado mixture. Add the shrimp and garnish with cilantro.

(19) Pumpkin, Coconut and Rum Soup

A hearty yet flavorsome soup for would-be pirate's intent on sailing the high seas. Perfect for a landlubbers get together too!

Yield: 6-8

Cooking Time: 9hours 20mins

List of Ingredients:

- 2 teaspoons vegetable oil
- 2 medium yellow onions (peeled, chopped)
- 2 garlic cloves (peeled, chopped)
- 1 bunch scallions (white and pale green parts, sliced)
- 2 pound pumpkin flesh (peeled, cut into 2 "cubes)
- 2 large carrots (peeled, thickly sliced)
- 1 Scotch bonnet pepper (stemmed, chopped)
- 6 cups chicken stock
- 1 (14 ounce) can coconut milk
- Sea salt and black pepper
- 1-2 tablespoons sugar (to sweeten, optional)
- ⅓ cup dark rum

MMMMMMMMMMMMMMMMMMMMMMMMMMMMMM

Methods:

1. In a heavy pot, over moderate heat, heat the oil.
2. Add the onions, frequently stirring, until they start to caramelize, this will take around 20 minutes.
3. Stir in the garlic along with the scallions and cook for 60-90 seconds, until soft.
4. Add the pumpkin along with the carrots, Scotch bonnet pepper, chicken stock, and coconut milk.
5. Bring to boil and reduce the heat to moderate to low.
6. While uncovered, simmer for between 30-40 minutes, until the veggies are soft and the liquid has slightly reduced.
7. Remove the pot from the heat, transfer to a food blender and process to a puree.
8. Return to the pot and stir in the sugar (to taste) along with a pinch of sea salt and a dash of pepper.
9. Pour in the rum and stir to combine.
10. Cover, place in the fridge, overnight.
11. When you ready to serve, reheat by boiling the soup vigorously for a few minutes.
12. Serve hot.

(20) Pirate Paté

When it's time to get your friends together for a parley and a party then this make-ahead chicken liver pate flavored with rum is sure to be a big hit.

Yield: 10-12

Cooking Time: 11hours 15mins

List of Ingredients:

- 3 shallots (thinly sliced)
- 1-pound chicken livers
- 6 sprigs of thyme (tips and leaves only)
- Water
- 2 pinches of salt
- 4 tablespoons unsalted butter
- Pinch of cinnamon
- 1 tablespoon dark rum

MMMMMMMMMMMMMMMMMMMMMMMMMMMMMM

Methods:

1. Over moderate to high heat, fry the shallots, chicken livers, thyme and ⅓ cup of water in a deep frying pan, bring to simmer.
2. Reduce the heat to moderate low and simmer for 3-5 minutes, until the chicken lives are sufficiently cooked through.
3. Transfer the mixture to a food blender.
4. Add the salt along with the butter, cinnamon and rum, and process until silky smooth.
5. Transfer the pate to ramekins and lightly cover with the kitchen wrap.
6. Transfer to the fridge, to chill, overnight.
7. Allow to stand at room temperature for 2-3 hours before serving.

Chapter III – Main Recipes

MMMMMMMMMMMMMMMMMMMMMMMMMMMMMM

(21) Yo Ho Ho Roast Rum Duck

Basting a whole duck with rum results in super juicy meat and a delicious golden coloring.

Yield: 2

Cooking Time: 2hours 30mins

List of Ingredients:

- 1 (5 pound) whole duck (cleaned)
- 2 tablespoons brandy
- 1 orange
- 1 yellow onion
- 1 garlic cloves (cruised)
- ¼ pound melted salted butter
- ½ cup rum
- ¼ teaspoons powdered ginger
- Salt

MMMMMMMMMMMMMMMMMMMMMMMMMMMMMM

Methods:

1. Preheat the main oven to 400 degrees F.

2. Place the bird in a roasting tin.

3. Soak a clean cloth in the 2 tablespoons brandy and use the cloth to wipe the bird's cavity.

4. Pierce, the whole outside of the orange and onion using a fork, and insert into the duck's cavity.

5. Truss the duck, and then rub the outside with the garlic clove and brush with melted butter.

6. Place the duck in the oven and cook for 15 minutes. Turn the temperature down to 350 degrees F and cook for another 1 hour 40 minutes.

7. Half an hour before the duck is due to be cooked, take out of the oven. Drain away any fat from the roasting tin. Pour the rum into the tin and baste the duck with the juices. Return to the oven and continue to baste at regular intervals.

8. Sprinkle the duck with ginger and salt before serving.

(22) Ahoy Me Hearties Beef Stew

After a busy day on the high seas or in the office, this hearty beef stew is a satisfying and warming meal!

Yield: 6

Cooking Time: 1hour

List of Ingredients:

- 3 rashers bacon (chopped)
- 2 pounds lean beef (cut into cubes, dredged in flour)
- 2 garlic cloves (peeled, diced)
- 1 yellow onion (peeled, diced)
- 1 green bell pepper (seeded, chopped)
- ⅓ cup golden rum
- 16 ounces canned whole tomatoes
- Splash Worcestershire sauce
- 1 bay leaf
- ½ teaspoons thyme
- Salt and black pepper
- 2 potatoes (peeled, cubed)
- 4 carrots (peeled, sliced)

MMMMMMMMMMMMMMMMMMMMMMMMMMMMMM

Methods:

1. In a Dutch oven over moderate heat, sauté the bacon until crisp.
2. Add the beef in batches, and cook until browned.
3. Add the garlic, onion, and bell pepper and cook until soft.
4. Pour in the rum and tomatoes and stir well. Season with a splash of Worcestershire sauce, bay leaf, thyme, salt, and black pepper.
5. Cover with a lid and cook for 45 minutes over low heat.
6. Uncover and add the potatoes and carrots, re-cover and cook for a final 20 minutes before serving.

(23) Sweet Potato and Rum Casserole

Sweet potatoes aren't just for Thanksgiving! This delicious vegetable is delicious all year round, especially when livened up with a good ol' glug o' rum.

Yield: 8-10

Cooking Time: 45mins

List of Ingredients:

- Butter (to grease)
- 1 cup granulated sugar
- 3 cups cooked sweet potato (mashed)
- 2 medium eggs (lightly beaten)
- 1 teaspoon vanilla essence
- ½ cup whole milk
- ½ cup melted butter
- ⅓ cup dark rum
- 1 cup pecans (chopped)
- 1 cup brown sugar
- ⅓ cup melted butter
- ⅓ cup self-raising flour

MMMMMMMMMMMMMMMMMMMMMMMMMMMMMMM

Methods:

1. Preheat the main oven to 350 degrees F. Grease a 13x9" baking dish.
2. Stir the sugar into the mashed sweet potatoes then stir in the beaten egg.
3. All at once, pour in the vanilla essence, milk, and ½ cup melted butter. Stir to combine then stir in the rum. Spoon into the baking dish.
4. Combine the pecans, brown sugar, ⅓ cup melted butter, and flour in a bowl. Sprinkle over the casserole.
5. Place in the oven and bake for half an hour. Set aside for 10 minutes before serving.

(24) Long John Silver's Battered Cod

These lightly-battered, golden pieces of cod are fit even for the most infamous of pirates such as Long John Silver himself.

Yield: 6-8

Cooking Time: 30mins

List of Ingredients:

- 8 cups oil (for deep frying)
- ¼ cup cornstarch
- 2 cups flour
- 2 teaspoons granulated sugar
- ½ teaspoons baking powder
- 2 teaspoons salt
- ½ teaspoons bicarb of soda
- ½ teaspoons onion salt
- ¼ teaspoons black pepper
- ½ teaspoons paprika
- 1 ounce rum
- 15 ounces soda water
- 2 pounds fresh cod (cut into 3 ounces pieces)

MMMMMMMMMMMMMMMMMMMMMMMMMMMMMM

Methods:

1. Heat approximately 8 cups of oil in a deep fryer to 350 degrees F.

2. In the meantime, prepare the batter. Combine the cornstarch, flour, sugar, baking powder, salt, bicarb of soda, onion salt, black pepper, and paprika in a bowl. Stir in the rum and club soda, do not worry if it foams.

3. Dip the pieces of fish in the batter mixture then drop into the hot oil and fry for a few minutes until golden.

4. Place the cooked fish on a wire rack to rest for 60-90 seconds before serving.

(25) Prawn and Chicken Rum Mango Curry

Pirates of the Caribbean will love the tropical flavors of this coconut prawn and chicken curry.

Yield: 4

Cooking Time: 8hours 40mins

List of Ingredients:

- Fresh thyme leaves
- 2 carrots (diced)
- 2 garlic cloves (peeled, crushed)
- 1 onion (peeled chopped)
- 4 chicken breasts (chopped)
- Black pepper
- 3½ teaspoons curry powder
- Canola oil
- 4 tablespoons rum
- 2 apples (cored, diccd)
- 1 cup coconut milk
- 1 cup chicken broth
- 1 tablespoon fresh coriander (chopped)
- 1 ripe mango (peeled, stoned, diced)
- 10 king prawns (peeled, veined)
- 2 tomatoes (deseeded, chopped)
- 1 tablespoon fresh parsley (chopped)
- Cooked white rice (to serve)

MMMMMMMMMMMMMMMMMMMMMMMMMMMMMMMM

Methods:

1. Toss together the thyme leaves, carrot, half of the garlic, half of the onion, and all of the chicken. Cover and chill overnight.

2. Uncover, add the remaining garlic and onion. Season with black pepper and curry powder.

3. In a pan over moderate heat, warm a drop of oil. Add the chicken and veggies, sauté for a few minutes until browned.

4. Stir in the rum and apples, cook for a couple of minutes until the rum cooks out.

5. Pour in the coconut milk and broth and bring to a boil. Turn the heat down to a simmer and cook for 10 minutes.

6. Add the coriander, mango, prawns, and tomatoes. Cook for a few minutes until the prawns are white through.

7. Garnish with fresh parsley and serve with rice.

(26) Balsamic-Glazed Rack of Lamb with Allspice and Rum

Ahoy me hearties! This fabulously meaty lamb dish is not one to be missed.

Yield: 4

Cooking Time: 30mins

List of Ingredients:

- 2 large, Frenched racks of lamb
- 1 teaspoon allspice
- Salt and black pepper
- 2 tablespoons good-quality balsamic vinegar
- 1 ounce brown sugar
- 2 tablespoons dark rum
- 1 ounce salted butter
- Mashed sweet potato (to serve)

MMMMMMMMMMMMMMMMMMMMMMMMMMMMMM

Methods:

1. Preheat the main oven to 450 degrees F.
2. Season the lamb on both sides with the allspice, salt, and black pepper. Arrange in a shallow dish.
3. Next, make the glaze. Combine the vinegar, sugar, and rum in a small bowl.
4. Pour the glaze over the lamb and set aside to marinate for half an hour.
5. Melt the butter in a large pan over moderate heat.
6. Remove the lamb from the marinade and brown in the pan for a few minutes on each side.
7. Place the browned meat in roasting tin and place in the oven. Roast for approximately 10 minutes until medium rare.
8. Serve with sweet potato mash.

(27) Maple and Rum Glazed Salmon

Whether you a salty seadog or landlubber, this sticky maple-glazed salmon will suit all taste buds.

Yield: 4

Cooking Time: 1hour 30mins

List of Ingredients:

- 2 tablespoons Dijon mustard
- ¼ cup maple syrup
- ¼ cup dark rum
- 4 (6 ounce) salmon fillets (boneless)

MMMMMMMMMMMMMMMMMMMMMMMMMMMMMMMM

Methods:

1. Combine the mustard, maple syrup, and rum in a shallow dish. Add the salmon and flip to evenly coat. Cover with plastic wrap and chill for an hour.

2. Preheat the main oven to 450 degrees F.

3. Take the salmon out of the marinade shaking off any excess and transfer to a glass baking dish. Place in the oven and bake for approximately 25 minutes until cooked through.

4. In the meantime, prepare the glaze.

5. In a small saucepan over moderately high heat, bring the marinade mixture to a boil. Turn the heat down to moderately low and simmer for 10 minutes until reduced.

6. Serve the cooked salmon with the glaze/sauce.

(28) Big Juicy Pirate Burgers

These devilish, cheese-stuffed burgers with spicy jerk seasoning, caramelized onions, grilled pineapple, and of course a good glug of rum, will appeal to all you outlaws who dare to do things a little differently.

Yield: 6

Cooking Time: 8hours 40mins

List of Ingredients:

Caramelized Onions:

- 1 tablespoon butter
- 1 tablespoon sugar
- 2 yellow onions (peeled, separated intoringsg)

Pineapple:

- 1 whole pineapple (peeled, cored, sliced into 6 rings)
- 6 tablespoons sugar

Burger:

- 1 cup canned black beans
- 2 cups cheddar cheese (shredded)
- 2 teaspoons BBQ seasoning
- 1 cup dried papaya (diced, soaked in water for several minutes, then drained)
- ¾ teaspoons allspice
- 3½ tablespoons golden rum
- 1½ tablespoons jerk seasoning
- ¾ teaspoons sweet paprika
- ½ teaspoons freshly ground black peppercorns
- ½ teaspoons salt

- 3 pounds ground beef
- 2 tablespoons canola oil
- 6 brioche buns (halved)

MMMMMMMMMMMMMMMMMMMMMMMMMMMMMMMMMM

Methods:

1. In a skillet over moderately low heat, melt the butter. Add the sugar and onions and sauté for approximately 20 minutes while occasionally stirring until softened and caramelized. Set to one side.
2. Next, prepare the pineapple. Sprinkle each pineapple ring on both sides with 1 tablespoon of sugar. Set to one side.
3. Next, make the stuffing. Combine the black beans, cheese, BBQ seasoning, papaya, allspice, rum, jerk seasoning, paprika, peppercorns, and salt in a bowl.
4. Preheat a gas grill to moderate heat.
5. Divide the beef into 6 portions and roll each into a ball then flatten into a disc.

6. Spoon a ⅓ of a cup of the stuffing mixture onto the center of each patty. Use cleans hands to form the meat around the stuffing, reforming a ball shape then patting again into a patty shape.

7. Place the patties on the grill and cook for approximately 8 minutes each side.

8. A few minutes before the burgers are done cooking, place the pineapple on the grill. Cook for a couple of minutes each side.

9. Place a patty inside each brioche bun and top with a slice of pineapple. Serve!

(29) Castaway BBQ Mackerel with Spicy Mango Rum Salsa

Cook this delicious whole fish dish the pirate way; outside on a BBQ! Alternatively, if you don't have a sandy beach and ocean side view pop it on the grill.

Yield: 4

Cooking Time: 1hour

List of Ingredients:

Salsa:

- 3 tablespoons rum
- 2 ounces fresh orange juice
- 1¼ ounces raisins
- 1 ripe mango (peeled, stoned, diced)
- 6 scallions (sliced)
- 1red chilii (deseeded, diced)
- 1 tablespoon fresh mint (chopped)
- 2 tablespoons fresh coriander (finely chopped)
- Juice of ½ a lime

Fish:

- 4 whole mackerel (cut horizontally on each side, don't cut through to bone)
- ½ teaspoons powdered ginger
- Juice of 2 medium limes
- 8 bay leaves
- 4 sprigs thyme
- 2 limes (sliced)

- 2 ounces olive oil
- Salt and black pepper

MMMMMMMMMMMMMMMMMMMMMMMMMMMMMMMMMM

Methods:

1. To a saucepan over moderately high heat, add the rum, orange juice, and raisins. Take off the heat and set aside to soak for half an hour.

2. Stir the diced mango into the raisin mixture followed by the scallions chili, mint, coriander, and lime juice. Set to one side until ready to serve.

3. Preheat your BBQ for grilling on high heat.

4. Season the inside and outside of the mackerel with the ginger and the juice of 1 lime.

5. Stuff each mackerel with 2 bay leaves, 1 thyme sprig, and a handful of lime slices. Allow to sit for 10 minutes.

6. Mix the remaining lime juice with the olive oil and a pinch each of salt and black pepper.

7. Arrange each fish on a large square of kitchen foil. Spoon over an equal amount of the lime-oil and make a parcel using the foil.

8. Place the parcels on the BBQ for approximately 10-12 minutes until the fish are cooked through.

9. Serve hot with prepared salsa.

(30) Buttery Rum Ham

This bountiful ham is cooked in a buttery rum glaze.
Perfect for even the biggest of appetites.

Yield: 8-10

Cooking Time: 1hour 30mins*

List of Ingredients:

- 2 tablespoons hot buttered rum batter
- 1 cup light corn syrup
- 1 tablespoon strong-brewed coffee
- ¼ cup golden rum
- 1 (9-12 pound) spiral bone-in ham

MMMMMMMMMMMMMMMMMMMMMMMMMMMMMMMM

Methods:

1. Preheat the main oven to 275 degrees F.
2. Combine the rum batter, corn syrup, coffee, and rum in a small bowl. Brush the glaze mixture over the ham.
3. Place the ham face down in a roasting pan and cover with foil.
4. Place in the oven and bake for 12-15 minutes for every pound.
5. Serve warm.

*Depending on the size of the ham.

Chapter IV – Dessert Recipes

MMMMMMMMMMMMMMMMMMMMMMMMMMMMMM

(31) Toffee-Coffee Cheesecake

An indulgent dessert, which combines the flavors of coffee tiramisu and tangy, sweet cheesecake. Perfect for any buccaneer bash!

Yield: 12

Cooking Time: 8hours 15mins

List of Ingredients:

- 4 tablespoons coffee-flavored liqueur
- 4 tablespoons dark rum
- 1¼ cups espresso (cooled)
- 7 ounces ladyfinger biscuits
- 8 ounces mascarpone cheese
- 8 ounces cream cheese (whipped)
- ½ cup granulated sugar
- 1 cup heavy whipping cream (whipped)
- 2 teaspoons baking cocoa
- ¾ cup toffee pieces

MMMMMMMMMMMMMMMMMMMMMMMMMMMMMMMM

Methods:

1. Combine 2 tablespoons liqueur, 2 tablespoons rum, and espresso. Pour the liquid into a shallow bowl.

2. Dip 12 of the ladyfinger biscuits in the liquid in the shallow bowl. Arrange the ladyfinger biscuits in the base of a 7x11" dish.

3. Beat together the mascarpone cheese, cream cheese, sugar, remaining 2 tablespoons liqueur, 2 tablespoons rum in a large bowl.

4. Fold a quarter of the whipped cream into the cheese mixture.

5. Spoon half of the mixture over the ladyfinger biscuits and use a spatula to smooth it out evenly. Sprinkle over 1 teaspoon cocoa and half of the toffee pieces.

6. Dip the remaining 12 biscuits in the reaming espresso mixture.

7. Using the remaining soaked biscuits, cheese mixture, cocoa powder, and toffee bits to repeat the same layers.

8. Cover with plastic wrap and chill overnight.

(32) Boozy Bananas Foster

Did you know that in the 18th century, at the height of the trading empire between the Caribbean and Spain that the majority of ships that disappeared were carrying bananas?

Yield: 5

Cooking Time: 2hours 10mins

List of Ingredients:

- 5 ripe bananas (halved crosswise then lengthwise)
- ¼ cup melted butter
- 1 cup brown sugar
- 1 teaspoon vanilla essence
- ¼ cup rum
- ½ teaspoons cinnamon
- ⅓ cup shredded, sweetened coconut
- ⅓ cup walnuts (chopped)
- Vanilla ice cream

MMMMMMMMMMMMMMMMMMMMMMMMMMMMMM

Methods:

1. Layer the banana in the base of a slow cooker.
2. Combine the melted butter, sugar, vanilla essence, rum, and cinnamon in a small bowl and pour the mixture over the banana. Cover and cook for 90 minutes until hot through.
3. Sprinkle over the coconut and nuts, cook for another half an hour.
4. Serve with vanilla ice cream.

(33) Rum 'n Raisin Crème Brulee

In the sugarcane rich Caribbean rum was easy to come by and this creamy brulee is pirate perfect.

Yield: 6

Cooking Time: 6hours 40mins

List of Ingredients:

- ¼ cup dark rum
- ⅓ cup raisins
- 2½ cups heavy whipping cream
- Yolks of 7 large eggs
- ½ cup + 6 teaspoons superfine sugar

MMMMMMMMMMMMMMMMMMMMMMMMMMMMMMM

Methods:

1. Preheat the main oven to 325 degrees F.
2. Combine the rum and raisins in a small bowl and cook in the microwave for 30-40 seconds. Allow to soak for 10 minutes.
3. In a small saucepan over moderate heat, warm the cream until bubbles. Take the pan off the heat.
4. Whisk the egg yolks and ½ a cup of sugar in a bowl until combined. Stir the hot cream into the egg mixture.
5. Strain the rum from the raisins into the cream mixture and stir. Set the raisins to one side.
6. Place 6 (6 ounce) ramekins in a large baking pan.
7. Divide the rum-soaked between the 6 ramekins and pour over the custard mixture.

8. Pour hot water into the hot pan so that it reaches within ¾" of the top of the ramekins.

9. Place in the oven and bake in the oven for just over half an hour until set.

10. Take the ramekins out of the water bath and set to one side to cool to room temperature. Transfer to the refrigerator for 4-6 hours.

11. Sprinkle 1 teaspoon of sugar over each cool custard. Use a kitchen blowtorch to caramelize the sugar until it bubbles and turns golden. Serve straight away.

(34) Brown Sugar Peaches in Rum Sauce

No self-respecting buccaneer would turn down sweet peaches in a rich rum sauce.

Yield: 6

Cooking Time: 2hours 10mins

List of Ingredients:

- ¼ cup unsalted butter
- ¾ teaspoons cinnamon
- 6 tablespoons brown sugar
- 6 ripe peaches (peeled, pitted, sliced into eighths)
- 2 teaspoons vanilla essence
- 2 tablespoons dark rum
- Vanilla ice cream (to serve)

MMMMMMMMMMMMMMMMMMMMMMMMMMMMMMM

Methods:

1. In a skillet over moderate heat, melt the butter.
2. Add the cinnamon and sugar, cook while stirring until the sugar dissolves.
3. Next, add the peaches and vanilla essence, cook for 4-5 minutes, occasionally tossing until the fruit has softened.
4. Take the skillet off the heat and stir in the rum. Return the skillet to the stovetop and cook for a couple of minutes more until the sauce thickens.
5. Serve with vanilla ice cream.

(35) Pecan and Pumpkin Bundt with Spiced Rum Glaze

Yo Ho Ho! this deliciously-flavored bundt cake will take your coffee break to the next level.

Yield: 12

Cooking Time: 1hour 30mins

List of Ingredients:

Cake:

- ½ cup pecans (chopped)
- ½ cup granulated sugar
- 1 (15 ounce) can pumpkin
- 4 large eggs
- ½ cup canola oil
- ¼ cup water
- ½ teaspoons nutmeg
- 1½ teaspoons cinnamon
- Pinch cloves
- 1 regular-size package yellow cake mix

Glaze:

- ½ cup salted butter (chopped)
- 1 cup granulated sugar
- ¼ teaspoons cinnamon
- Pinch cloves
- ½ cup dark rum

MMMMMMMMMMMMMMMMMMMMMMMMMMMMMMM

Methods:

1. Preheat the main oven to 350 degrees F. Butter and flour a 10" bundt tin. Scatter the chopped pecans in the base of the tin and set to one side.
2. Beat together the sugar, canned pumpkin, eggs, oil, and water in a bowl.
3. In a second bowl, combine the ground spices and cake mix.
4. Beat the cake mix into the pumpkin mixture a little at a time until incorporated.
5. Pour the batter into the bundt tin.
6. Place in the oven and bake for just under an hour until cooked through. Allow to cool to warm before glazing.
7. To make the glaze, place a saucepan over moderate heat. Melt together the butter, sugar, and spices.
8. Take off the heat and stir in the rum. Return the pan to the stovetop and cook for a couple more minutes until thick.
9. Brush the glaze onto the warm cake a little at a time, allowing each layer of glaze to soak in before applying more.
10. Allow the cake to completely cool before serving.

(36) Heavenly Vanilla and Rum Mousse

Just one mouthful of this super fluffy and air-light vanilla rum mousse won't transport you to Davy Jones' locker but it will take you to cloud nine!

Yield: 8

Cooking Time: 2hours 20mins

List of Ingredients:

- ¼ cup water
- 1 tablespoon gelatine
- 2 cups whole milk
- 1 teaspoon vanilla essence
- ¾ cup granulated sugar
- Yolks of 6 eggs
- 1 tablespoon dark rum
- Ice
- 1½ cups heavy cream (whipped)

MMMMMMMMMMMMMMMMMMMMMMMMMMMMMMM

Methods:

1. Add the water to a small bowl and sprinkle over the gelatine and set aside for 5-6 minutes.
2. Heat the milk and vanilla essence in a saucepan over low heat until hot through.
3. In a clean bowl, whisk together the sugar and egg yolks. Whisk the hot milk mixture into the egg yolks a splash at a time.
4. Return the milk and egg mixture to the saucepan and cook over low heat, while continually stirring until the mixture is nice and thick.
5. Take the pan off the heat and pour the mixture into a large bowl. Add the gelatine and whisk to combine. Add the rum and stir.
6. Make an ice bath and place the bowl of custard mixture in the ice bath to cool until the custard mixture is almost set.
7. Fold in the whipped cream until just incorporated.
8. Spoon into small glasses or bowls and chill for a couple of hours before serving.

(37) Orange and Spiced Rum Bread Pudding

Shiver me timbers! This boozy bread pudding has a delicious squishy texture and spiced rum sauce.

Yield: 12

Cooking Time: 1hour 15mins

List of Ingredients:

- Butter (for greasing)

Pudding:

- 1 (17 ounce) pound cake (cut into 1" cubes)
- 1½ cup whole milk
- 5 medium eggs
- ¼ cup granulated sugar
- ½ cup fresh orange juice
- 1 teaspoon vanilla essence
- 1 tablespoon good-quality spiced rum
- ½ cup brown sugar

Sauce:

- ¼ cup salted butter
- ¼ cup good-quality spiced rum
- Zest of 1 medium orange
- ½ cup granulated sugar
- Pinch each nutmeg, cinnamon, allspice
- 1 cup whip topping

Methods:

1. Grease an 11x8" baking dish. Arrange the cubes of cake in the base of the dish. Set to one side.

2. Preheat the main oven to 350 degrees F.

3. Add the milk, eggs, granulated sugar, orange juice, vanilla essence, and rum to a large bowl and whisk to combine.

4. Pour the mixture over the cake in the dish. Allow to soak for 15 minutes. Sprinkle over the brown sugar.

5. Place in the oven for just over 35 minutes until the custard has set. Take out of the oven and keep warm while you prepare the sauce.

6. In a saucepan over moderate heat, add the butter, rum, orange zest, sugar, and spices. Stir and bring to a gentle boil. Turn down to a simmer. Pour in the whipped topping and whisk to combine.

7. Take off the heat. Serve the sauce with the bread pudding.

(38) Hummingbird Cake with Cream Cheese Rum Frosting

Sea biscuits were hard cookies, which pirates would eat on long journeys thanks to their 12-month shelf life. This deliciously moist and tropical hummingbird cake could not be further from those crunchy little biscuits, but it does have pirate-approved rum buttercream!

Yield: 8-10

Cooking Time: 1hour 30mins

List of Ingredients:

- Butter (to grease)

Cake:

- ⅓ cup corn oil
- 1 cup granulated sugar
- 1 teaspoon vanilla essence
- 2 medium eggs
- 1 teaspoon bicarb of soda
- 1½ cups flour
- ¾ teaspoons powdered ginger
- 1 teaspoon baking powder
- 8 ounces canned, crushed pineapple
- ½ cup macadamia nuts (chopped)
- ½ cup shredded coconut

Buttercream:

- 3 tablespoons butter
- 3 ounces full-fat cream cheese
- 2 cups confectioner's sugar
- 1 tablespoon dark rum
- 1½ teaspoons vanilla essence

- ¼ cup macadamia nuts (chopped)
- ¼ cup toasted coconut flakes

MMMMMMMMMMMMMMMMMMMMMMMMMMMMMMMMMM

Methods:

1. Preheat the main oven to 350 degrees F. Grease a 9" square cake tin.
2. Combine the oil, sugar, vanilla essence, and eggs in a bowl,
3. Combine the bicarb of soda, flour, ginger, and baking powder in a second bowl.
4. Mix the dry mixture into the wet mixture a little at a time until incorporated.
5. Fold in the pineapple, macadamia nuts and coconut.
6. Pour the batter into the cake tin.
7. Place in the oven and bake for just over half an hour. Allow to cool completely before frosting.
8. To make the frosting, beat together the butter and cream cheese in a bowl. Add the confectioner's sugar a little at a time until incorporated. Stir in the rum and vanilla essence, followed by the chopped nuts and coconut flakes.
9. Frost the cooled cake with the buttercream, slice, and serve.

(39) Jamaican Rum Truffles

Jamaica was once pirate central with Port Royal being its capital. Here, pirates such as Calico Jack, Henry Morgan and Blackbeard all walked its streets. These indulgent, rum-infused chocolate truffles are a true taste of the Caribbean.

Yield: 36

Cooking Time: 8hours 20mins

List of Ingredients:

- 14 ounces semi-sweet chocolate
- 1 cup heavy cream
- 1 teaspoon spiced rum
- ⅓ cup salted butter (at room temperature)
- ½ cup toasted pecans (finely chopped)

MMMMMMMMMMMMMMMMMMMMMMMMMMMMMM

Methods:

1. Set aside 2 ounces of chocolate. Roughly chop the remaining chocolate.
2. Add the cream to a saucepan and heat until it just begins to bubble. Take off the heat and add the chocolate, stir well until the chocolate completely melts. Allow to cool.
3. Add the rum and butter to the melted chocolate and stir to combine. Cover with plastic wrap and chill overnight.
4. Grate the set-aside chocolate and add to a small dish with the pecans.
5. Use a tablespoon to scoop the chilled chocolate mixture into round balls. Roll each ball in the grated chocolate and nuts.
6. Keep chilled until ready to enjoy.

(40) Iced Mango, Rum, and Coconut Pudding

You will have no trouble getting everyone on board when you serve this creamy rum pudding.

Yield: 8

Cooking Time: 30mins

List of Ingredients:

- 9 ounces dried mango (chopped)
- 4 tablespoons dark rum
- 4 ounces golden superfine sugar
- Yolks of 4 eggs
- 12 ounces cream
- 4 ounces creamed coconut (grated)
- 7 ounces Greek yogurt
- Mango and passionfruit puree

MMMMMMMMMMMMMMMMMMMMMMMMMMMMMM

Methods:

1. Soak the mango and rum in a small bowl for a few hours.
2. Whisk together the sugar and egg yolks.
3. In a saucepan over low heat, bring the cream to a gentle boil.
4. Pour the cream into the bowl of egg yolks whisking continually.
5. Pour the combined mixture into the saucepan and return to the heat. Gently cook until the mixture warms. Take off the heat.
6. Stir in the grated coconut. Allow to completely cool before stirring in the yogurt and rum soaked mango, along with the rum.
7. Line a loaf tin with kitchen wrap and pour in the pudding mixture.
8. Freeze overnight before serving with mango and passion fruit puree.

About the Author

A native of Indianapolis, Indiana, Valeria Ray found her passion for cooking while she was studying English Literature at Oakland City University. She decided to try a cooking course with her friends and the experience changed her forever. She enrolled at the Art Institute of Indiana which offered extensive courses in the culinary Arts. Once Ray dipped her toe in the cooking world, she never looked back.

When Valeria graduated, she worked in French restaurants in the Indianapolis area until she became the head chef at one of the 5-star establishments in the area. Valeria's attention to taste and visual detail caught the eye of a local business person who expressed an interest in publishing her recipes. Valeria began her secondary career authoring cookbooks and e-books which she tackled with as much talent and gusto as her first career. Her passion for food leaps off the page of her books which have colourful anecdotes and stunning pictures of dishes she has prepared herself.

Valeria Ray lives in Indianapolis with her husband of 15 years, Tom, her daughter, Isobel and their loveable Golden Retriever, Goldy. Valeria enjoys cooking special dishes in her large, comfortable kitchen where the family gets involved in preparing meals. This successful, dynamic chef is an inspiration to culinary students and novice cooks everywhere.

•••••••••••••••••••••••

Author's Afterthoughts

Thank you for Purchasing my book and taking the time to read it from front to back. I am always grateful when a reader chooses my work and I hope you enjoyed it!

With the vast selection available online, I am touched that you chose to be purchasing my work and take valuable time out of your life to read it. My hope is that you feel you made the right decision.

I very much would like to know what you thought of the book. Please take the time to write an honest and informative review on Amazon.com. Your experience and opinions will be of great benefit to me and those readers looking to make an informed choice.

With much thanks,

Valeria Ray

Printed in Great Britain
by Amazon